GITHUB AND GIT

A BEGINNER'S GUIDE TO GIT AND GITHUB

BY

JEFFREY DAHMER

Table of Contents

INTRODUCTION

Hello and welcome to the Git and GitHub repositories! This project will teach you all you need to know about Git, a powerful tool for recording changes in your coding projects, and GitHub, a popular site for collaborating and sharing code with others.

Git keeps track of any changes you make to your code, allowing you to quickly monitor and manage multiple versions of your project. With Git, you can test new features, correct issues, and roll back changes as required, all while keeping a clean and structured history of your code.

GitHub, on the other hand, offers a platform for hosting your Git repositories and allows you to collaborate with other developers in real time. You may share your code, contribute to open-source projects, and get community comments.

Git is a great tool for tracking changes in coding projects and collaborating with others. It's like a magical notepad that enables us to collaborate on projects while tracking who made what changes and when.

WHY DO WE NEED GIT?

We need Git because it makes coding projects simpler and less complicated to work on. Here are a few reasons why Git is fantastic:

Tracking Changes: Git allows us to keep track of all changes. the adjustments we make to our code. It's as if we had a time machine that could transport us to any version of our application. Assume you're writing on an essay and want to see what it looked like last week. Git can provide the precise version of your writing from that point in time.

Collaboration: Git enables us to work together on the same code project as others. Git, like working on a group project in school, allows each participant to work on their side of the program without interfering with each other. It helps us prevent disagreements and makes combining everyone's work simpler. Assume you and your buddies are working on a tale together. Git guarantees that everyone's modifications are synchronized. are well-organized and seamlessly integrated into the overall tale.

Branching and merging: There are instances when we wish to try out new features or repair issues without disrupting the main application. Git allows us to set up a distinct workspace called a "branch" where we may work on these concepts. If things don't go as planned, we can quickly return to the main program without incident. Once the branch's modifications are complete, they may be simply merged back into the main codebase. This entails merging the successful improvements from the isolated branch into the main project. Assume you have a lovely garden and wish to experiment with various sorts of flowers in a specific area. Branches enable you to try new things. without interfering with the rest of the garden. Merging is similar to taking lovely flowers from a separate portion of your yard and placing them in the main garden to make it more vivid and diversified.

Reverting Changes: Git allows us to rectify errors or problems in our code. It's almost as if we had a "undo" button for our modifications. If we discover a mistake, we may quickly revert to a prior version and begin again. Assume you're sketching a picture and you inadvertently make an erroneous stroke. Git enables you to undo that stroke and start again from scratch.

Code Checks: Git works well with websites like GitHub, where we can share our code and learn from others' efforts. We can We may show off our coding abilities, get criticism, and even contribute to open-source projects. It's similar like joining a large community of hackers and studying with them. Assume you're a member of a book club where everyone shares their favorite novels. Git and GitHub are similar systems that enable programmers to exchange and learn from one another's work.

WHAT EXACTLY IS GIT?

Git is a tool that assists us with version control, which is the process of keeping track of all the changes we make to our code over time. It's like a magical notepad that keeps track of all of our coding efforts.

We utilize Git to capture snapshots of our project at various periods in time. These snapshots are known as "commits." Each commit denotes a distinct version of Our endeavor. Assume you're working on an art project and taking pictures of your work every time you complete a step. Each image symbolizes a commitment, displaying the evolution of your artwork over time.

Git is also "distributed," which means that each developer has their own copy of the whole project, including all changes. It's similar to having your own copy of the artwork with all of its images on your computer. This way, you can work on the project even when you're not connected to the internet, and when you're finished, you can share your modifications with others. It's similar to showing your artwork to your pals so they can view the various stages and give suggestions.

to make it even better Git makes it easier to construct distinct "branches" of our project. These branches are similar to different narratives or versions of our project. Assume you and your buddies are working on a fantasy narrative. Git allows each user to establish their own branch so that they may work on various chapters or characters without becoming confused. When everyone is satisfied with their modifications, Git may integrate the several branches and merge them into a single final tale.

To summarize, Git is a magical notebook that organizes our coding projects, facilitates cooperation, and helps us become superhero programmers!

GIT BASIC COMMANDS

Are you ready to become a Git expert? Here are some fundamental Git commands that make you feel like a code superhero:

'git init': Assume you're beginning a new project. A new coding journey. The 'git init' operation is analogous to packing your luggage for a trip. It creates a new Git repository, which will be used to monitor your code modifications.

clone git: Assume your buddy has a fantastic project to which you'd want to contribute. The git clone command is equivalent to copying their project to your machine. It's similar to taking a book from a friend's library to read and take notes on.

git add: Consider the git add command to be similar to putting items in your rucksack. It's similar to adding code files or modifications to the staging area, preparing them for the next phase.

git push: You've finished a job or made a change to your code. The git's The commit command is equivalent to taking a picture of your work and storing it along with a message. It's similar to marking a milestone in your journey, enabling you to look back and realize how far you've gone.

git status: Curious about what's going on with your code? The git status command acts as a map, indicating where you are in your coding journey. It informs you of which files have changed, what is ready for commit, and any outstanding tasks.

Consider your project to have numerous narratives or avenues to investigate. You may establish distinct narratives or branches with the git branch tool. It's similar to picking multiple adventure tracks to work on different features or test out new ideas.

git check-in: Assume you're working on many branches or desire to revert back to an earlier version of your code. The git checkout command is like to shifting gears in your trip. It lets you move between branches and go back in time to earlier versions of your project.

git merge: Working with others is an interesting aspect of coding. The git merge command merges several branches or stories. It's like bringing together people from diverse travels and combining their tales into one.

Let's imagine your pals have been working on the project and you want to see the most recent modifications. The git pull command is analogous to obtaining an update package. It downloads the most recent code from a remote repository and incorporates it into your project.

git commit: Finally, you are pleased with your job. I'd want to share it with others. The git push command is like to posting your experience online for anyone to see. It commits your modifications to a remote repository, making them available to others.

You are now ready to begin your coding adventures with Git! Investigate these commands, try out various branches, and cooperate with others.

CREATING A REPOSITORY

To begin utilizing Git for version control in your project, first create a repository:

Launch your favourite terminal program, such as Terminal on macOS or Command Prompt on Windows.

Go to the Project Directory: Look for the folder containing your project files. It's like discovering a hidden entry to your coding journey.

Create the Repository: Use the In your terminal or command prompt, type the magic words git init. It's similar like casting a spell on your project directory to establish a new Git repository.

Gather All of Your Magical Files: Collect all of the files you wish to put in your repository. To add them one by one, use the command git add filename>. It's similar to gathering magical objects and preparing them for your journey.

Commit Your Changes: Use a custom message to capture the current status of your project. To make your first commit, use git commit -m "Initial commit". It's the same as putting your magical things in a treasure box and writing a letter explaining why.

Remote Repository (Optional): If you want to share your coding magic with others or retain a backup, here is the place to do it. Create a remote repository in the cloud using services like as GitHub, GitLab, or Bitbucket. It's similar to having a hidden magical castle where you can keep your spells.

You have successfully created a Git repository for your project by following these instructions. You may now use Git to monitor changes, create branches, and collaborate with others.

WRITING EFFECTIVE COMMIT MESSAGES

It is critical to write clear and detailed commit messages in order to collaborate effectively and have a clean commit history. Here are some pointers to help you construct effective commit messages:

Make Your Commitment Message simple and Concise: Make your commit message simple and concise. To define the aim of the commit, use straightforward and explicit language. Avoid communications that are unclear or ambiguous since they might cause misunderstanding.

Separate the subject and the body of your commitment: message with a topic and, if required, a body. The topic should be a succinct description (typically 50 characters or fewer) of the commit's core point. The body may supply further information or explanations.

Begin with an Imperative Verb: To express what the commit accomplishes, begin the subject line with an imperative verb. Use terms like "Add," "Fix," "Update," and "Refactor." This contributes to the clarity and uniformity of your commit statements.

Explain why the commitment is required and offer important background. Describe the problem or issue at hand, as well as how the commit resolves or improves it. This helps others comprehend the commitment's purpose and effect.

Maintain Relevance: Concentrate on the precise modifications made in the commit. Include no unrelated modifications or specify every file that is impacted. Maintain the emphasis of the commit message on the core aim of the commit.

Maintain Good Grammar and Punctuation: Use proper grammar, spelling, and punctuation in your commit messages. This improves both readability and professionalism. To guarantee correctness, review your messages before committing.

Commit messages should be written in the present tense, as though you were explaining the current status of the codebase. For example, say "Fix a bug" rather than "Fixed a bug." This gives the impression of uniformity and clarity.

Consider the 50/72 Rule: Keep your commit messages to a subject line of 50 characters and a body of 72 characters. This guarantees that messages may be read in a variety of circumstances, such as in Commit logs or web interfaces are examples of such places.

Refer to Relevant Issues: Include a reference to a relevant issue or feature request in the commit statement. For example, "Fix #123" may be used to relate the commit to issue number 123. This aids in the tracking of changes and gives more context.

evaluate and amend: Before committing, evaluate and amend your commit message. Make certain that it appropriately communicates the changes and adheres to the principles outlined above. Taking the time for this step guarantees that your commit history is clear and meaningful.

Remember that excellent commit messages increase teamwork and help others understand the context and intent of your changes. In your commit messages, strive for clarity, relevancy, and professionalism.

WORKING WITH BRANCHES

The branch is a pointer to a specific commit in your commit graph, also branches are used to track the version of your code.

As we know the master(main) branch is the stable version of your code, so isolating it from any new feature until it has been tested and agreed to be used in your code, you can merge it.

The git branch command has four main usages which are(list/create/update/delete):

things to keep in mind when working with branching:

Branch name should be descriptive and easy to remember.

It is a good practice to create branches based on the feature or bug you are working on.

You can have multiple branches open at the same time.

You can switch between branches at any time.

How can I create an effective README?

When generating project documentation in README.md, it's critical to develop a resource that's clear, thorough, and user-friendly. Good documentation assists developers and end users in successfully understanding, using, and contributing to the project.

Before we get into the specifics, let's put some markers on the table to indicate who and what:

What exactly is your project?

What exactly does it do?

Who is it intended for?

Tips

Consider the following suggestions for writing an outstanding README:

Use Simple words: Explain complicated ideas in simple words. It's like using familiar terms to guide explorers through a mysterious place.

Structure: Divide your information into distinct parts. It's similar to writing separate chapters for a fascinating novel.

Maintain a consistent style and formatting throughout your work. README. It's similar to keeping the enchantment of your journey.

Updates: As your project changes, keep your README up to date. It's like adding additional chapters to an ongoing story.

You may get ideas from other projects on GitHub by looking at how they format their READMEs.

Improve your Productivity by updating your.gitconfig file.

The insteadOf directive in the.gitconfig file instructs Git to rewrite any URL that begins with a certain string to begin with a different string.

[url="https://github.com"] as an example

     git@github.com insteadOf

This instructs Git that if you clone a repository with a URL that begins with https://github, Git should rewrite the URL to begin with git@github instead.

This manner, you can always use SSH to clone the repository. Enter the incorrect URL.

The insteadOf directive is useful for rewriting URLs for any domain.

In our instance, the problem is the token, which we use every time we clone a repository or give a remote URL that includes your token.

For instance, supposing you were cloning your repo using:

https://YOUR_PERSONAL_TOKEN@github.com/YOUR_USERNAME/alx-zero_day.git clone

The second method is to use the git command:

https://YOUR_PERSONAL_TOKEN@github.com/YOUR_USERNAME/alx-zero_day.git git remote set-url origin

We saw how you fixed it in the previous example, but now we're going to alter the.gitconfig to enable Git to add our token anytime we clone or init any repo.

Navigate to the root and list all files and folders, even those that are hidden.

For instance, root@190347384:# ls -al -rw-r--r-- 1 root root 152 Sep 2 06:56 .gitconfig Look for the '.gitconfig' file after listing all the files and folders.

Open the.gitconfig file in your favorite text editor, such as vi, emacs, or nano, and add the following:

[url "YOUR_PERSONAL_TOKEN@github.com/"]

rather than = https://github.com/

By adding these two lines, git will no longer prompt you for login credentials, but it will save your personal access token in your repository config file and utilize it to let you to seamlessly push and pull in any feature project.

HAPPY CODING AND GIT EXPLORATIONS!

Remember that with Git at your side, you're ready to tackle any coding difficulty and work with other engineers. May your commits be significant, your branches be productive, and your merges be smooth. Continue to explore, learn, and share your coding magic with the world. I wish you the best of luck and fun on your coding path!